TO ALL THE BRACKENS— ESPECIALLY THOSE BORN IN A TRUNK

THE PALACE

ANIMAL CRACKERS

A Menagerie of Jokes and Riddles

Illustrated by Carolyn Bracken

Platt & Munk, Publishers/New York
A Division of Grosset & Dunlap

Library of Congress Catalog Card Number 78-68414. ISBN 0-448-46531-0 (Trade Edition); ISBN 0-448-13071-8 (Library Edition)

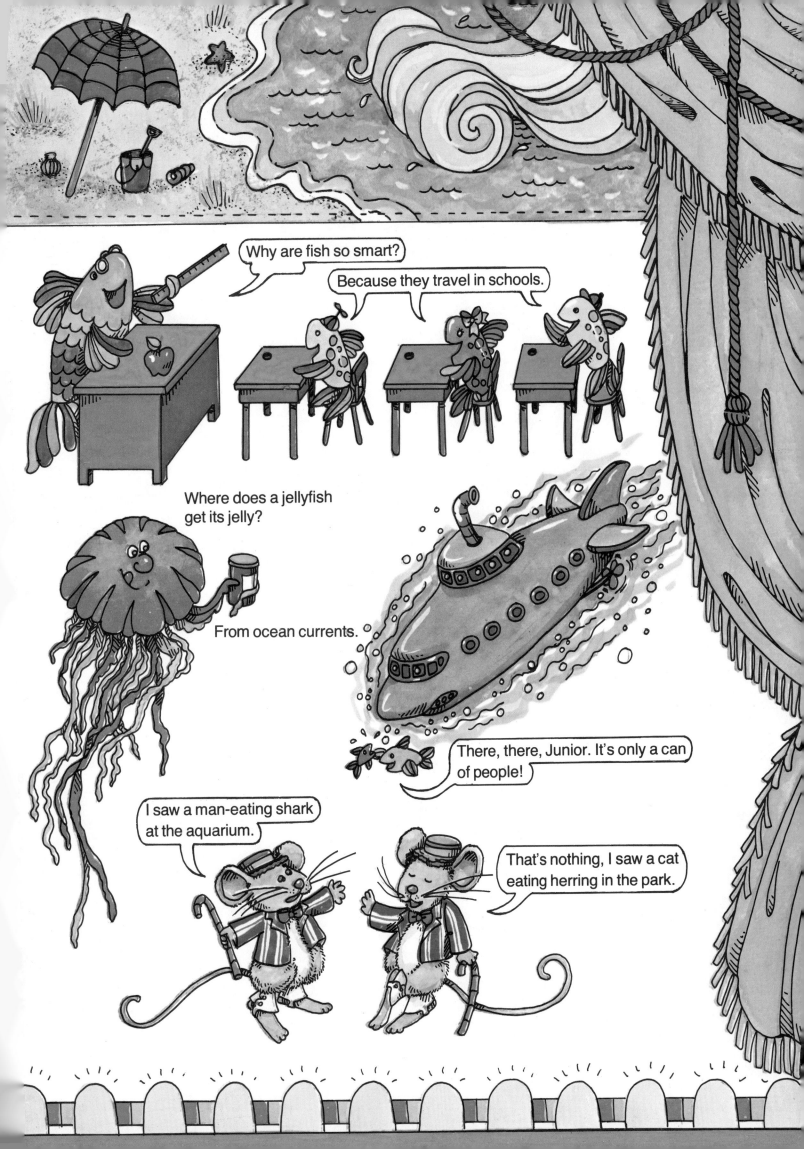